Calmness

PRANAY

BUDDHA
WISDOM LIBRARY

Published by

FiNGERPRINT!
Prakash Books

Fingerprint Publishing
@FingerprintP
@fingerprintpublishingbooks
www.fingerprintpublishing.com

ISBN: 978 93 6214 311 2

Remembering our Buddha-nature
makes us calm.

OM MANI PADME HUM

Let go of what has passed,
Let go of what may come!
Let go of what is happening now!
Do not try to figure anything out . . ...
Do not try to make anything happen.
Relax right now, and rest!

—The '6 Rules' of the Mahasiddha Tilopa
(the great master of Mahamudra,
Tantra and Vajrayana Buddhism)

Rest in the lowest place,
and you will reach the highest!

—Milarepa, the great MahaYogi
of Tibetan Buddhism

Contents

Section 1

Section 2

Section 1

Buddhist Principles
for Calmness

CHAPTER 1

The Buddha Symbolizes Serenity

The Buddha embodies the most profound calmness and the ultimate serenity. He is the foremost symbol of the tranquil dynamism inherent in existence.

The timeless wisdom of Buddhism remains profoundly relevant in our fast-paced world. It poignantly reminds us to slow down, embrace tranquility, remain calm, and fulfill our lives through a state of stillness and peaceful contentment. Calmness is both the path and the means to enlightenment.

Buddhist teachings resonate deeply with modern psychology and neuroscience, offering profound insights into the nature of consciousness. By quieting the mind from the distractions of worldly pursuits, we uncover deeper truths and experience heightened awareness and bliss.

Buddha imparted the wisdom that unrest in the mind inevitably leads to suffering, while tranquility and inner peace pave the way to true joy. At the heart of Buddhism lies cultivating a serene and focused mind, fostering equanimity, emotional composure and mental repose amidst life's myriad challenges.

Buddhism venerates relaxed mental clarity, facilitating genuine calmness, self-discovery, and inner peace. Its message transcends specific beliefs, emphasizing the universal importance of nurturing a tranquil consciousness. Through this understanding, one can attain authentic success, self-realization, and profound joy.

ESSENTIAL TEACHINGS FOR INNER CALMNESS

The Essence of Mental Tranquility

The Buddha imparted the most profound wisdom for mental calm. He taught the deepest methods for attaining the tranquil, composed, centered state of being (signified by the Pali words *passaddhi* and *samatha*). Buddha's teachings underscore the importance of diminishing the cacophony of thoughts within our minds.

In Buddhism, the optimal state of mind is likened to a serene lake devoid of ripples. We are encouraged to cultivate such tranquility, quietness, and unperturbed composure. By quieting the mind, one attains the clarity to perceive reality as it truly exists. At the core of Buddhism lies this deep insight into the nature of reality.

Ethical Conduct and Virtuous Behavior

The Buddha emphasized the significance of morality and virtuous behavior, known as *abhisamacharika-shila* in Buddhist terminology. Genuine, pure conduct is essential for fostering a tranquil demeanor, as it leads to a positive state of mind and consciousness.

In the *Appamāda Sutta*, the Buddha elucidated: 'Monks, there are four instances where heedfulness should be exercised. Which four? Abandon bodily misconduct, cultivate good bodily conduct: Do not be heedless there. Abandon verbal misconduct and cultivate good verbal conduct: Do not be heedless there. Abandon mental misconduct and cultivate good mental conduct: Do not be heedless there. Abandon the wrong view, cultivate the right view: Do not be heedless there.'

A life rooted in mindfulness and ethical conduct lays the foundation for acquiring insight, leading to inner serenity. This inner peace, in turn, fosters right conduct and thoughts, settling the mind into a state of tranquility, calmness and a resolute commitment to do what is righteous. This forms the cornerstone for nurturing a virtuous temperament and attaining profound wisdom.

Love and Serenity in Buddhist Philosophy

Central to Buddhism is the profound notion of loving kindness, known as *metta*. Buddhism recognizes that loving kindness engenders tranquillity. Loving kindness expands our self-awareness and amplifies the power of the heart, naturally fostering calmness.

The essence of the Buddha's teachings fundamentally revolves around love and its blossoming within us. Significantly, all Buddhist meditative practices are meticulously crafted to guide us toward embracing love, perceived as the ultimate reality of existence in the Buddhist worldview.

The Essence of Silence

At the heart of Buddhism lies the simplicity and elegance embodied in the act of quiet sitting alone in contemplation (*ekasanam*). This practice quiets the mind, bestowing it with peace.

Through this meditative practice, one establishes a profound connection with the present moment and attains a state of perfect calmness. The very essence of seated silence encapsulates the core of Buddhist meditation.

Revealing Inner Tranquility

In Buddhism, the profound lesson lies in shedding our attachment to selfhood (*attabhava*) and delving into the essence of our existence. At this core, beyond name and form, lies perfect calmness. In exploring our depths, we also begin to perceive our Buddha-nature (BuddhaDhatu).

By awakening to the inner sanctuary of our potential Buddhahood, we grasp the essence of the Buddha's teachings and their profound wisdom.

Rediscovering Our Natural State of Being

Buddhism revolves around the journey back to our natural state—the unconditioned essence of our being, characterized by innate calmness. In this state, we can directly perceive the luminosity of existence and experience profound relaxation.

According to Buddhist philosophy, we enter life in pristine purity, but societal influences and thoughts gradually shape us. The crux of Buddhism lies in returning to our natural, unblemished selves—a rediscovery of childlike wonder and authenticity. This teaching illuminates the profound Buddhist wisdom regarding our inherent nature.

Navigating Challenges: The Path to Growth and Serenity in Buddhism

In Buddhism, challenges are viewed not as obstacles but as opportunities for personal evolution. Embracing this perspective, we should never fear or shy away from challenges. To genuinely evolve and attain true serenity, we must confront challenges directly, embodying the courage akin to that of the Buddhas.

Those following the Buddha's path embrace all fears, thus achieving fearlessness and calmness. By confronting challenges head-on, we cultivate the capacity to transcend them, advancing our journey toward spiritual growth and inner tranquility.

Nirvana: Liberation, Freedom, and Enlightenment in Buddhism

The Buddha used the word 'nirvana' (nibbana in Pali) to describe spiritual realization and enlightenment, signifying complete cessation, unbinding, liberation, and freedom. In Buddhism, enlightenment symbolizes liberation: freedom from our limited concepts, freedom from our fears, freedom from the restless, agitated mind, and freedom from the illusion of our non-Buddha nature.

It embodies absolute calmness intertwined with boundless bliss. This profound understanding grants us genuine freedom, tranquility, and spiritual awakening.

Expressive Stillness:
The Wisdom of Body Language

In Buddhism, the symbolism conveyed through statues holds profound significance, as the depicted body language is a profound teacher, guiding us on how to carry ourselves.

The statues of the Buddha are iconic representations of the state of inner peace. While the hustle and bustle of our daily lives often leave us restless, statues depicting the Buddha radiate an aura of perfect calm, inward relaxation, serene demeanor, joy, and a spontaneous sense of enlightenment. By drawing inspiration from the tranquil body language portrayed in Buddha statues and delving into their deeper messages, we can cultivate a profound sense of calmness and collectedness within ourselves. This understanding empowers us to refine our body language, not only enhancing our composure but also enabling us to effortlessly convey tranquility to everyone we encounter, leaving us utterly relaxed.

Embracing Equanimity: Buddhist Wisdom in Times of Loss and Death

In the face of loss, grief often envelops us in profound emotional turmoil and confusion. However, from the Buddhist perspective, navigating the journey through loss and confronting the inevitability of death (*marana*) can be best approached through meditation.

This practice grants us a heightened awareness of the cycles of life and death, leading us to a state of equipoise and genuine balance, allowing for a confrontation with reality. Meditating upon death becomes a profound opportunity for enlightenment in Buddhism. Embracing a meditative outlook toward death unveils the greatest potential for spiritual awakening and authentic understanding.

Understanding Aparigraha: The Principle of Non-accumulation

At the core of Buddhist philosophy lies the profound concept of non-accumulation, known as aparigraha.

Non-accumulation transcends the mere gathering of material possessions; it extends to refraining from accumulating excessive ideas, thoughts, and conditioned views.

Buddhism advocates for the relinquishment of these burdens. Letting go of attachment to material possessions is significant, yet shedding false notions and perceptions is paramount.

By releasing these mental constructs, truth and serenity arise effortlessly and organically.

CHAPTER 2

The Six Perfections: Pathways to Serenity and Enlightenment

Buddhism introduces the Six Perfections, also known as the Six *Paramitas*, as guiding principles toward serenity, calmness, and enlightened living. Let us delve into these transformative qualities:

1. **Generosity:** Embracing generosity transcends egocentric mentalities, liberating our minds and souls from the shackles of self-centeredness.
2. **Ethics:** The second perfection entails living ethically and honestly, aligning with one's highest self. Ethics foster discipline, virtue, and profound serenity within.
3. **Patience:** Infinite patience, exemplified by bodhisattvas, leads to the realization of boundless bliss and the expression of limitless compassion.
4. **Enthusiastic Perseverance:** True perseverance, fueled by enthusiasm, becomes the driving force behind achieving worldly endeavors while maintaining inner calmness.
5. **Concentration:** The fifth perfection is calm concentration, akin to a focused beam of light or a laser beam, which manifests great capabilities and accomplishes remarkable feats.
6. **Pure Wisdom:** The final perfection is pure wisdom, untainted by anxiety or tension. This radiant wisdom, akin to bodhisattvas and Buddhas, renders one spontaneously serene and utterly calm, akin to the tranquil depths of an unaffected ocean beneath the rolling waves.

Embracing these Six Perfections leads to a transformative journey toward enlightenment and a serene existence.

CHAPTER 3

Meditative Absorption for Inner Calmness: Exploring Jhana

Tilopa, the renowned master of Indian and Tibetan Tantra, aptly stated: 'It is not the outer objects that entangle us. It is the inner clinging that entangles us.'

At the heart of Buddhism's teachings on calmness lies the concept of Jhana, or meditative absorption, which naturally fosters tranquillity, relaxation, and profound calmness.

Jhana is the cornerstone of Buddhist practice, offering pathways to mental, emotional, and spiritual tranquility. Particularly, Samatha meditations, also known as tranquility meditations, are revered as potent tools for achieving calmness from a Buddhist perspective.

Four types of Jhanas exist, each representing varying levels of calmness, culminating in complete tranquility of sensory activity and unveiling the mind's true nature of absolute lucidity and calmness. The initial Jhana is associated with profound delight and forms part of refining consciousness, leading to a lucid, alpha state of mind. While some Jhanas are rooted in material experiences, others transcend the material realm, delving into pure consciousness and infinite space, where perceptions and non-perceptions cease to exist.

Jhana embodies self-purification, immersion in a state of insight where one attains complete unity with universal concepts and achieves profound nobility, compassion, and spiritual liberation. According to Buddhist doctrine, all mystical aspirations hinge on meditation, particularly the practice of Jhana. Buddhism underscores the practical application and cultivation of appropriate meditation techniques to facilitate personal metamorphosis.

In Buddhism, a plethora of meditation techniques exist, including Gautam Buddha's personal meditation known as Anapanasati Yoga. This practice simply involves observing the breath going in and out—it is accessible to all and offers the path to calmness at any moment.

Despite the diversity of practices, certain foundational principles are emphasized across various meditation techniques, notably the eight meditative absorptions or Jhanas:

1. **Detachment from Unwholesome Thoughts and Experiencing Joy (*Sukha*):** Letting go of unwholesome thoughts leads to the experience of joy.

2. **Quieting Thoughts and Achieving Inner Tranquility, Leading to Joy:** Quieting the mind brings inner peace and joy.

3. **Establishing Clarity, Equanimity, and Mindfulness, Leading to Absorption:** Cultivating clarity, equanimity, and mindfulness leads to absorption.

4. **Transcending Pleasure and Pain, Cultivating Equanimity (*Upekkha*):** Rising above pleasure and pain cultivates equanimity.

5. **Transcending Perceptions of Matter and Senses, Realizing Boundless Space:** Moving beyond perceptions of matter and senses reveals boundless space.

6. **Recognizing the Boundless Nature of Consciousness and Dwelling Within It:** Realizing the infinite nature of consciousness and dwelling within it.

7. **Realizing the Essence of Non-Existence, Entering the Sphere of Nothingness:** Understanding the essence of non-existence leads to the realm of nothingness.

8. **Transcending All Mental Conditioning, reaching a State Beyond Perception and Non-Perception, Leading to Profound Tranquility and Bliss, Moving Toward Enlightenment:** Rising above all mental conditioning leads to a state beyond perception and non-perception, characterized by profound tranquility and bliss, propelling one toward enlightenment.

Understanding and practicing these various absorptions and meditations are essential for attaining true tranquility and calmness in life, per Buddhist teachings.

CHAPTER 4

Wisdom from Buddhist Scriptures

*Victory breeds hatred; the defeated
live in pain. The peaceful live happily
giving up victory and defeat.*

Gautam Buddha

B uddhist scriptures delve deep into describing the factors that enable us to lead tranquil, calm, and happy lives. Yet, Buddhism's beauty lies in its ability to summarize these key factors into understandable and tangible concepts.

For instance, Buddhism outlines the 25 wholesome or *kushala* factors, which pave the path towards great equanimity. Among these 25 wholesome factors are the 19 Sobhanasadharana, or 'universally splendid mental factors,' which include:

1. **Faith:** Having confidence or faith, known as *Saddha* in the language of Pali.
2. **Mindfulness:** Cultivating mindfulness, referred to as *Sati* in Pali.
3. **Decency:** Upholding decency, known as *Hiri*.
4. **Modesty:** Practicing modesty, called *Ottappa*.
5. **Non-greed:** Letting go of greed, known as *Alobha*.
6. **Non-hatred:** Abandoning hatred, referred to as *Adosha*.
7. **Equanimity:** also known as *Tatramajjhattata*, fosters balance and impartiality in our outlook.
8. **Tranquillity of Thoughts:** also known as *Kayapassadhi*, entails a serene state of mind, free from agitation.

9. **Tranquillity of Consciousness:** also known as *Chittapasadhi*, signifies a calm and serene consciousness.

10. **Lightness of the Mental Body:** this quality also known as *Kayalahuta*, reflects a lightness of being, devoid of burdensome attachments.

11. **Lightness of Consciousness:** also known as *Chittalahuta*, denotes a light and unburdened state of consciousness.

12. **Malleability of the Mental Body:** this quality also known as *Kayamuduta*, indicates a flexible and adaptable mental disposition.

13. **Malleability of Consciousness:** also known as *Chittamuduta*, signifies a pliable and adaptable consciousness.

14. **Wieldiness of the Mental Body:** also called *Kayakammanata*, this quality, denotes a skillful and adept mental disposition.

15. **Wieldiness of Consciousness:** also known as *Chittakammannata*, it reflects a skillful and adept consciousness.

16. **Proficiency of the Mental Body:** also known as *Kayapagunattha*, this quality, signifies a proficient and capable mental disposition.

17. **Proficiency of Consciousness:** also known as *Chittapagunnata*, denotes a proficient and capable consciousness.

18. **Rectitude of the Mental Body:** also known as *Kayujukata*, this quality, signifies an upright and honorable mental disposition.

19. **Rectitude of Consciousness:** also known as *Chittujukata*, denotes an upright and honorable consciousness.

Moreover, Buddhism teaches us the principles of Karuna, or compassion, and Mudita, or empathetic joy. Cultivating these qualities within us leads us spontaneously to Paññā or wisdom, facilitating a life of profound calmness, tranquillity, and serenity.

Buddhism also cautions against the 14 unwholesome or *Akushala* factors that veer us from serene living. These detrimental factors are:

1. **Delusion:** also known as *Moha* in Pali, delusion clouds our understanding and perception.

2. **Lack of Shame or Decency:** also known as *Ahirika*, denotes a lack of moral conscience.

3. **Lack of Modesty:** also called *Anottappa*, signifies a lack of humility or modesty.

4. **Restlessness:** also known as *Uddhacca*, denotes a state of agitation and unease.

5. **Greed:** also known as *Lobha*, denotes fostering of insatiable desires and attachment.

6. **Wrong Views:** also called *Ditthi*, signifies wrong views lead to misguided beliefs and perceptions.

7. **Pride:** also known as *Mana*, breeds arrogance and conceit.

8. **Hatred:** also known as *Dosa*, signifies hatred, engenders animosity, and hostility.

9. **Envy or Jealousy:** also known as by *Irsya*, breeds resentment and discontent.

10. **Selfishness:** also known as *Macchariya*, prioritizes personal gain over the welfare of others.

11. **Excessive Worry:** also known as *Kukkucca*, leads to anxiety and distress.

12. **Laziness:** also known as *Thina*, hampers productivity and growth.

13. **Torpor:** also known as *Middha*, manifests as lethargy and sluggishness.

14. **Skepticism or Doubt:** also known as *Vicikiccha*, undermines confidence and clarity of mind.

Avoiding these unwholesome factors paves the path toward a life imbued with inner tranquillity. Our thoughts, emotions, and actions gradually quieten, resonating with the strength of silence within. This progression propels us toward Nirvana or *Nibbanna*, the state of complete calm and peaceful enlightenment envisioned by the Buddhas.

Section 2

Buddhism's Insights and
Secrets for Calmness

CHAPTER 5

The Wisdom of the Authentic Self

The essence of Buddhahood lies in embracing your most authentic being, as you truly are (*yathatatha*). From the Buddhist perspective, being your authentic self means recognizing that you do not need to strive to *become* something; you *already embody* the essence of what you seek to become!

Such natural authenticity leads to understanding yourself and the power which resides within you, which in turn leads to a feeling of rootedness, stillness, and calm self-dignity.

The secret to true tranquility and composure indeed lies in realizing your *actual being*. This teaching encourages an understanding that authenticity is the path to genuine peace within oneself.

DISCOVERING SERENITY: EMBRACING THE INNER WITNESS IN BUDDHISM

In the Buddhist perspective, the Buddha resides as the inner witness (*sakkhi*) within you—a consciousness observing everybody action and thought of the mind, yet distinct from both body and mind.

Deepen your connection with this inner witness within you to unravel the profound tranquility of being a serene Buddha. It creates infinite contentment and quietness within you.

THE CHOICELESS WATCHER: EMBRACING EQUANIMITY IN BUDDHISM

In Buddhism, the ideal mindset is of the choiceless watcher. This state is compared to a person who is observing weather fluctuations, from sunny moments to rainy ones, yet who maintains an unwavering choicelessness!

Cultivate this mindset with a calm and non-reactive alertness.

Then, you can transcend life's ever-changing circumstances with serene calmness, unwavering poise, unyielding courage, boundless bliss, and enduring joy.

UNCONDITIONAL LOVE: THE ESSENCE OF JOY IN BUDDHISM

A genuine Buddhist harbors love without any specific cause, drawing from an abundant inner wellspring of love, expressing it simply for the sake of love.

This perspective, accompanied by a sharing attitude, brings a sense of radiant joy, tranquility, meditation, and devotion.

Embracing the attitude of unconditional love not only enriches one's life with profound joy but also radiates that joy to others.

TRANSCENDING BOUNDARIES: THE CORE OF BUDDHIST WISDOM

Central to Buddhism is the recognition that you extend beyond the constraints of body and mind; your essence is that of a limitless Buddha. Expanding your vision of your true nature makes you calmer and quieter.

Connect with this infinite aspect of yourself to achieve excellence in life, genuine composure, and authentic self-confidence.

VITALITY UNLEASHED: THE POWER OF MEDITATIVE LIVING IN BUDDHISM

From the Buddhist perspective, the key to profound energy and vitality in effort (*ussaha*) lies in wholeheartedly dedicating yourself to meditative practices. The true idea of meditation is beyond *any particular seated meditation: it encompasses adopting a meditative attitude itself.*

Direct your complete energy toward cultivating this attitude and mindset, and you will find your intelligence becoming razor-sharp.

You will experience a heightened sense of aliveness and profound composure, unlocking the boundless vistas of life.

TRANQUIL WISDOM: EMBRACING THE ESSENCE OF COOLNESS IN BUDDHISM

At the heart of Buddhism lies the wisdom to cool the mind. In the hustle of life, our minds can become frantic, neglecting the need to unwind.

The Buddhist mind embodies completely cool calmness (*sitalatta*), akin to the soothing waters of a stream or a mountain lake.

Cultivate this serene quality within yourself, and you will discover profound self-strength.

CHAPTER 6

Eternal Essence: Unveiling the Teaching on the Buddhas

In Buddhism, the Buddhas transcend individual personalities. Gautam Buddha, though human, possesses a quality beyond his specific mortal existence. Buddhahood is an eternal essence woven into the fabric of existence, the core of the cosmic matrix.

This eternal quality extends to all, independent of the flesh-and-blood 'human' Buddha. Recognizing this unveils a broader vision, guiding one serenely toward the journey of becoming a Buddha oneself. One has to absent one's sense of mortality and identify with the no-mind, no-body state of pure consciousness.

THE TEACHING OF STILLNESS AND TRUTH

Buddhahood implies not *thinking* about truth but coming face to face with it through meditation. In the Buddhist vision, only the perfectly still and expansive mind can grasp greater truth, not the mind buffeted by thought.

Truth that is merely *thought about* will always be a half-truth or a lie.

Truth exists as a stream of reality, and the Buddhist is awake to the stream of reality. Therefore, he is able to grasp the truth as it is. And that is very empowering, very liberating. It creates profound peace of mind, expansion of consciousness, and a gentle yet massive strength of rootedness to the universe.

REFLECTIVE BONDS: WISDOM FROM JIDDU KRISHNAMURTI

Renowned mystic philosopher Jiddu Krishnamurti emphasized that relationships function as mirrors—reflecting our true selves. He was echoing the ancient teachings of the Buddhas. It is indeed through our interactions with others that we are mirrored.

Therefore, always be calmly vigilant in your relationships—infusing them with qualities such as peace, integrity, trust, love, and compassion.

Once nurtured, these virtues will resonate back to you in manifold ways, enriching the tapestry of your connections and making you serene and strong.

RADIANT LIVING: EMBRACING EMPATHY AND COMPASSION

Empathy (*anukampa*) and compassion (*daya*) breathe life into the noblest part of our being. True living is found in empathy and in compassionately relating to others.

Possessing these qualities infuses your entire life with spiritual bliss and a joy that transcends material possessions, creating a fulfilling and meaningful existence.

The energies of empathy and compassion generate an effortless ease.

SCULPTED STRENGTH: LESSONS FROM THE BUDDHA'S PERSONA

Observing any well-crafted statue of the Buddha reveals a unique blend of calming softness (*maddava*) and profound strength (*bala*) within his persona.

In our ordinary world, we often associate strength with a certain hardness, yet the Buddha exemplifies how a gentle, calm, and soft being can embody true strength.

The Buddha demonstrates infinite power resides in being soft and sensitive from within, coupled with unwavering resolution and determination.

Cultivate a strength akin to the Buddha's—soft, calm, fully resolved and unshakable.

COURAGEOUS SOLITUDE: NAVIGATING THE BUDDHA'S PATH

A fundamental quality for a true follower Buddha of Buddha's path is the courage to stand alone, calm and composed. The Buddha's wisdom emphasized that while walking with a suitable companion on the path is beneficial, genuine strength lies in the ability to move forward independently—you are enough unto yourself.

Therefore, do not be disheartened if someone from a past relationship is no longer walking beside you.

The power to walk alone is profound; it magnifies the flame of Buddhahood within you, bringing forth your greater qualities. As also echoed by the great Indian poet Rabindranath Tagore in his poem "*Ekla Cholo Re*" ('Walk on Alone!') . . .

HARMONY WITHIN: BUDDHA'S LESSON ON RECONCILING FAMILY BONDS

On the Buddha's path, reconciliation with family holds immense importance. Reconciliation creates serenity. It unlocks higher consciousness and clears the mind's horizons.

Even Gautam Buddha faced anger from his family upon visiting those years after his enlightenment. Despite their initial resentment, he, with a heart free of rancor, brought about harmony within their hearts and minds. Realizing his truer and greater purpose, his family, including his father, wife, and son, found a beautiful accord.

Similarly, we must approach our families with gentleness, recognizing the necessity of certain actions to fulfill our life's purpose. A lingering sense of unrest persists until we bring about harmony with our loved ones—an insight reflected in modern Freudian psychology. And Buddha stands as the ultimate teacher of psychology, ever; psychoanalysts would do well to learn from the depths of Buddhist teachings.

BEYOND DUALITIES: NAVIGATING THE PATH OF THE TRUE BUDDHA

On the path of the Buddha, true enlightenment lies in transcending the polarities of like and dislike. The practitioner is to watch the mind, witnessing all its likes and dislikes, till these concepts stop having a hold on one.

Despite our strong preferences in life, the Buddha encourages us not to be overly attached to them. Going beyond these dualities, treating both likes and dislikes with equanimity and calmness transforms our relationships and stabilizes us.

A profound change occurs within us by respecting those with different views. It helps us become more objective in our perception.

Hence, avoid excessive distinctions between preferences and people you like or dislike and instead foster an egalitarian approach. This approach, essential in today's world, benefits not only oneself but also others.

Buddhism, rooted in pursuing individual and collective well-being, seeks harmony within the individual and the environment.

CHAPTER 7

The Power of Discipline: Nurturing Inward Freedom in Buddhist Monastic Life

Within Buddhist monastic life, a multitude of rules and disciplines exist not to confine but to foster inward freedom. Discipline is a necessary adjunct to a calm, meditative life.

Acknowledging that genuine spiritual achievements arise from discipline, Buddhist rules and guidelines aim at creating an integrated and serene sense of being.

Embracing discipline is paramount. We must enjoy life's pursuits *while forging a resolute internal discipline.* This commitment ensures that our actions emanate with integrity, value, and purpose— embodying the core principle of purposeful living at the heart of Buddhism.

BEYOND MATERIAL PURSUITS: THE ESSENCE OF TRUE HAPPINESS IN BUDDHISM

At the core of Buddhist philosophy lies the profound notion that true peace of mind, bliss, and happiness cannot be purchased in the market. While many seek happiness through achievements like power, fame, and wealth, the challenge arises when we tether our happiness to these external factors.

Buddhism emphasizes that creating value and being productive are commendable, but the essence of true peace of mind, happiness, bliss, and enlightenment lies in the quality of one's being. Shift your focus to cultivating this quality by awakening your power of calm and patient perception.

This creates genuine and lasting happiness, transcending the dependency on external possessions.

THE ART OF DEEP LISTENING: A NOBLE TRAIT IN BUDDHISM

A distinctive quality of the true Buddhist is to master the art of receptive listening (*shravana*) with greater depth, attention, and profoundness. In a world filled with talkers, the profound insights of listeners often shine through. Deep listening, reminiscent of the followers of Buddha who absorbed his teachings, opens up an awakening within, calming and soothing us.

Cultivate this skill to align with those Buddhist masters who, through profound listening, progressed toward enlightened and noble living.

THE ESSENCE OF TRUE HUMILITY: A GUIDING PRINCIPLE IN BUDDHISM

For the true Buddhist, humility (*nihatamānatā*) is not a mere pretension but a manifestation of genuine integrity.

Cultivate humility from the deepest recesses of your heart and mind, embracing it as the path of the Buddha. True humbleness generates powerfully calm energy, fostering enlightened, fulfilled, and productive living. It serves as a means to eliminate unnecessary complexities from our lives, allowing us to live more simply and authentically, becoming true benefactors to others.

LIBERATING THE MIND: THE BUDDHA'S PATH TO PURITY

The wisdom of the Buddha lies in refraining from imposing anything upon the mind. Our rigid prejudices and views often burden the mind, diminishing its purity and creating restlessness or disturbance.

Conversely, Buddhism is a journey of freeing the mind of all external factors, freeing it from dogmas and misplaced beliefs, thereby creating expansiveness and restfulness within it.

By liberating the mind from self-imposed constraints, one breaks the chains that bind and attains the purity of Buddhahood.

ANCIENT WISDOM, MODERN VALIDATION: BUDDHISM'S INSIGHT INTO MIND POTENTIAL

Centuries before neuroscientists confirmed the underutilization of our brains, Buddhism espoused the idea that we tap into only a fraction of our mind's vast consciousness. The core of Buddhism revolves around attaining completely serene wakefulness and restful clarity, enabling the mind to realize its full potential.

Lucidity, synonymous with calm clarity, is pivotal. We unlock the mind's greater potential by consciously clearing and calming our minds through the meditatively wakeful attitude.

It is now essential to enhance our understanding of the profound wisdom embedded at the heart of Buddhism's teachings on the mind. Buddhism's insights into the alpha state of mind are remarkably resonant with today's neuropsychology and brain science (especially brain mapping).

THE PROFOUND ART OF ACCEPTANCE: BUDDHISM'S PATH TO EQUANIMITY

At its essence, Buddhism encourages the acceptance (*paṭiggahana*) of good and bad, evil and godly, profane and holy. Through complete acceptance, one attains a profound depth, becoming more capable of absorbing the deeper aspects of existence.

The Buddhist way advocates seeing through the eyes of absolute nonjudgmental openness until one achieves complete equanimity and calmness.

THE POWER OF PERSONAL TRANSFORMATION

Discovering your own Buddhahood is the most impactful way to benefit the world. This teaching echoes the wisdom of the Buddha.

While many aim to do good and help others, the highest form of goodness is striving toward personal perfection. Through that effort, our actions naturally become a service to humanity.

Buddhism tells us how individual enlightenment serves the greater good. The path to profound inner and outer peace is, hence, not separate from the path to enlightenment.

CHAPTER 8

Harmony in Understanding: Bridging Science and Buddhism

While science meticulously dissects the proportions of matter and energy, Buddhism takes a different path. Buddhahood asserts that life's meaning lies in the poetic equilibrium between your self-energy and cosmic energy.

Attaining this equilibrium and balance transforms you into moving toward Buddhahood, granting insight not only into your truths but also unraveling the mysteries of the universe for you.

The essence lies in the harmonious interplay of personal and cosmic energies, which creates a bridge between scientific analysis and Buddhism's profoundly calming wisdom.

RADIANT BUDDHAHOOD: CULTIVATING A POSITIVE AURA

Buddhahood unfolds as the transformative practice of crafting a positive energy field around oneself, radiating positivity to all. Often overlooked, each person carries profound energy fields shaped by thoughts, feelings, and overall energy.

Through intentional cultivation, embracing blissful states of *ananda* (delight, joy or *sukha*)—individuals naturally foster a positive energy aura. This spontaneous creation of positivity enriches personal experience and renders individuals charismatic and magnetically attractive to others.

Power lies in acknowledging and channeling the transformatively serene energy inherent in the pursuit of Buddhahood.

BUDDHIST SERENITY: EMBRACING POSITIVITY AND DISCARDING NEGATIVITY

A true hallmark of Buddhists is their ability to refrain from carrying negativity in their hearts and minds.

This liberation from negativity releases fears, apprehensions, anxiety, and stress. Buddhism, inherently life-positive, provides no space for negativity; adherents are encouraged to drop all negative aspects from their lives.

In a world saturated with negativity from news, entertainment, and our surroundings, Buddhists must possess the capacity to absorb yet not carry these burdens in their hearts or minds.

This message is at the heart of the Buddha's transformative vision: avoid negativity and embrace serenity.

THE ESSENCE OF PATIENCE IN BUDDHISM: A GATEWAY TO BUDDHAHOOD

At the heart of Buddhist philosophy lies the message of patience. The power of patience, *khantibala,* is an enduring virtue that encourages individuals to move through life with calmness and unhurried grace.

This idea finds eloquent expression in Zen Buddhism, which proclaims that all good things come to the patient, while impatience gives birth to folly.

According to Zen wisdom, patience strengthens one from within one's core, thereby allowing the seeds of Buddhahood to flourish.

Embracing patience becomes a transformative journey, leading to the realization of the inner Buddha nature within oneself.

PATH OF SELF-DISCOVERY: BUDDHISM'S AUTHORITY OF PERSONAL TRUTH

One of Buddhism's greatest virtues is its rejection of rigidly authoritative doctrines. The Buddha's core message emphasizes that the only genuinely authoritative doctrine is within oneself. He urges individuals to uncover their truths. His scriptures and words serve as directional pointers rather than dogma.

The essence of Buddhahood is indeed realizing oneself, thereby forging a unique path toward personal realization of cosmic reality.

Buddhism is a sublime religion, granting the authority for each individual to find their distinctive path to serenity.

THE ESSENCE OF INTELLIGENCE (*PAÑÑA*) IN BUDDHISM

In Buddhism, intelligence (*pañña*) is the refinement of purity and innocence. Cultivating mental purity and innocence draws one closer to the intelligence, serenity, stability, and unshakable composure embodied by the Buddha.

Conversely, cultivating cunning and cleverness moves you away from Buddhahood.

The essence lies in purity and innocence, rooted in a certain simplicity. Embracing simplicity makes us feel relaxed and more authentic to our true selves.

CHAPTER 9

Meditation in Buddhism: A Bridge to Cosmic Consciousness

In Buddhism, meditation serves as a bridge connecting oneself to the consciousness of the cosmos, the divine. It is not an end but a means—a powerful bridge that helps you reach the other side, symbolizing a transformative journey in Buddhist philosophy.

In Buddhism, meditation serves as a channel from our current state of mind toward our serene higher being.

As the Buddhist scriptures emphasize, "The mind is everything. What you think you become."

Now, meditation may seem like sitting in stillness, but it is a revolutionary activity, facilitating the transformation of mind and heart. Truly walking the path of the Buddha involves this profound journey of self-evolution through the practice of meditation.

THE ART OF BEING: UNIQUENESS IN BUDDHIST MEDITATION

Buddhist meditations stand apart by guiding individuals to relax into their being, fostering a state of complete composure.

These unique practices aim not for a specific end but a state of no end—a return to nothingness (*shunyata*).

The essence of Buddhist meditations lies in bringing individuals back to themselves, emphasizing the potent power of utter relaxation into their being.

Unlike seeking a particular goal, the focus is on rediscovering the self and facing reality with a composed and relaxed presence.

HARMONY IN THE SMALLEST ACTS: EMBRACING BUDDHAHOOD THROUGH METICULOUS ATTENTION

In the profound vision of Buddha, the intrinsic value of the smallest acts and things is paramount. Contrary to the misconception that Buddhahood demands grand endeavors, its essence lies in dedicating our calm and composed attention to the minutiae and executing them with the fullness of our energy.

This commitment transforms life into a symphony of joy and bliss.

Attuning ourselves to the smallest details unites us with the vastness of the divine and cosmic existence.

Embrace and respect the small things; the universe reciprocates manifold with universal energy and cosmic joy.

THE COSMIC SYMPHONY: DISCOVERING INFINITY IN THE MINUTE

Modern science unveils a profound insight—within the tiniest quantum particles resides an immense energy and intricate design, a blueprint for the entire cosmic existence. This revelation aligns with a fundamental aspect of Buddha's teachings—that within the small resides the infinite!

Indeed, to understand the grand, we must devote ourselves to comprehending the small.

By embracing the path of paying attention, being open, and listening with correct perception to the smallest details, we unravel the secrets of the universe. In this understanding of the smallest and greatest, one naturally embarks on the journey toward Buddhahood.

BUDDHA'S COURAGE: EMBRACING THE WARRIOR'S WAY

The path of the Buddha intricately weaves together true composure and courage—a philosophy often likened to the way of the warrior.

While Buddha advocated nonviolence, the core of the courage he sought to instill becomes apparent upon closer inspection. In Japan, even revered samurai warriors held deep respect for the principles of Buddha and often meditated (becoming composed and shedding the ego) before entering battle.

As Buddha emphasized, shedding the ego dispels fear, revealing a natural reservoir of empowered energy. True courage, according to Buddha, lies in facing reality as it is—an art that involves confronting everything without anxiety.

Buddha's teachings persist as a timeless example, urging us to confront challenges with unwavering strength, bravery, and resolve. We are to comprehend the essence of the Buddha through composure, courage, and calm resilience.

BUDDHA'S REVELATION: FINDING TRUE SATISFACTION IN THE MEDITATIVE JOURNEY TO ENLIGHTENMENT

The Buddha's profound teaching asserts that external pursuits cannot provide lasting satisfaction.

True contentment is discovered in the meditative state, the heightened awareness of ourselves, and the enlightenment that unites us with infinity—connecting us to stars, planets, cosmos, leaves, flowers, waterfalls, animals, and the breathtaking beauty of the universe.

This transformative journey begins with a meditative attitude, challenging the misconception that material accumulation leads to fulfillment.

In today's materialistic world, the Buddha's timeless message remains sublime. It reminds us that authentic satisfaction emanates from the inner journey. It underscores the essential wisdom that, irrespective of our pursuits, true contentment blossoms when we progress toward Buddhahood and embrace the meditatively composed state of being.

A JOURNEY OF INTEGRITY AND GRATITUDE

The Buddha told his disciples, "Now, what is the level of a person of no integrity? A person of no integrity is ungrateful and unthankful. This ingratitude, this lack of thankfulness, is advocated by rude people. It is entirely on the level of people of no integrity. A person of integrity is grateful and thankful. This gratitude, this thankfulness, is advocated by civil people. It is entirely on the level of people of integrity."

We can see that gratitude (called *Kataññu* in the Buddha's language of Pali) is key to the path of the Buddha. The grateful and non-envious mindset resonates with the inherent wisdom interwoven in Buddhist philosophy.

Acknowledging the profound value of our own existence and refraining from envy paves the way for an utterly calm and serene life. Such a life holds the innate potential to align with Buddhist teachings and reach the enlightened state of a Buddha.

Frequent comparisons with others often trigger ego-driven emotions—we feel hurt when we perceive ourselves as less and unwarranted superiority when we believe ourselves to be superior. In Buddhism, these attitudes are recognized as unwise and counterproductive.

The crucial shift begins with cultivating gratitude for our unique selves and appreciating the gifts we have received. Rooted in self-respect, this perspective sets the stage for a transformative journey toward embodying the state of a Buddha, reflecting the profound wisdom embedded in the teachings of Buddhism.

BUDDHIST COMMUNION:
THE ESSENCE OF
SHARING AND CARING

The Buddha said to his disciples, "Monks, there are two kinds of gifts: a gift of material things and a gift of the Dhamma. Of these two kinds of gifts, a gift of the Dhamma is supreme. There are two kinds of sharing: sharing of material things and sharing of the Dhamma. The supreme among these two kinds of sharing is the sharing of the Dhamma. There are two kinds of assistance: assistance with material things and assistance with the Dhamma. Of these two kinds of assistance, assistance with the Dhamma is supreme."

Central to Buddhism is the ethos of sharing and caring, epitomized in Buddha's commune (known as the *Sangha*).

A fundamental tenet is sharing spirituality, our innate energies, and possessions, as this creates internal bliss. Sharing one's best energies with others is a costless act that enriches not only their lives but also infuses one's existence with profound and blissful energy. This practice is the surest way to purify and cleanse oneself at the very roots, propelling individuals toward the transformative journey of moving closer to the sublimely calm and composed state of Buddhahood.

THE RESILIENT MIND: EQUANIMITY (*UPEKKHĀ*) VIA THE BUDDHIST PATH

From an authentic Buddhist perspective, complaining and succumbing to feelings of despair are eschewed. The true Buddhist embraces happiness and sorrow, pain and pleasure, with equal poise and understanding. The ideal Buddhist mindset is of great equanimity, resilience, and stoicism.

Such a mature mindset avoids distraction by new sensations or entertainment, remaining anchored in a balanced state.

Unaffected by the extremes of pleasure or dejection from pain, the Buddhist recognizes these diverse experiences as integral steps in the journey toward Buddhahood.

BECOMING EMPTY FOR BUDDHAHOOD: SHEDDING THE NOTIONS OF SELF

The Buddha instructed his beloved disciple Ananda (encapsulated within the *Suñña Sutta* or the *Sutra of Emptiness):*

"The mind is empty of a self or anything regarding a self."

In Buddhism, the path to becoming a Buddha requires completely emptying the sense of self. Holding onto ideas about one's identity impedes the realization of Buddhahood. To attain this state, one must relinquish the concept of being a physical being with a limited personality.

Recognizing oneself as pure awareness and consciousness creates space within, allowing the wisdom of the Buddha to take root.

The dissolution of the ego occurs when the understanding of pure awareness replaces self-identification. Negating oneself from preconceived notions and self-impressions opens the door to establishing Buddha's wisdom within.

Emptying the mind of imagined thoughts and personal narratives allows one to unburden oneself from one's own ideas about self, creating a lighter, more relaxed, and liberated state of being.

CHAPTER 10

Unlocking Inner Treasure: The True Path of the Buddha

I n the narrative of so-called civilization, the *pursuit* of material accumulation is heralded as the key to fulfillment. However, the path of the Buddha redirects our focus, asserting that true treasures lie within us. We must stop *pursuing*—and begin *realizing*—the treasure within us. This deeply relaxes us, making our energy completely dynamic.

Rather than relying on external allurements like material possessions and entertainment, the Buddha's path emphasizes the luminosity and serenity emanating from our own innate Buddha being.

Understanding this truth opens our hearts and minds to a different perception, bringing forth immense joy, increased energy, peace of heart, and unleashing our potential as creators of value in the world.

According to this philosophy, true success lies in realizing the brilliance within.

Even during the Buddha's lifetime, kings and princes, possessing everything, sought His guidance. Despite their wealth and dominion, they felt darkness within. The Buddha's teachings aimed to illuminate the inner lamp and dispel this internal darkness.

The analogy of lighting the lamp from within resonates throughout Buddhism, emphasizing the concentration on nurturing the inner light (which shows us our inner treasures) as both the means and the ultimate goal on the path of the Buddha.

WE ARE ABOVE OUR THOUGHTS

True wisdom arises from recognizing that we are above our thoughts. Our spiritual essence transcends our thoughts. Our inherent nature is loftier and nobler than the thoughts that often consume us.

In conventional terms, we tend to identify ourselves with our thoughts, diminishing our true stature in our self-consciousness. The essence of Buddhism lies in the profound teaching that we should not attach ourselves to our thoughts; instead, we should realize that from the spiritual perspective, we stand far above the realm of our thoughts.

This shift in perspective brings great clarity and balance to our lives and cultivates genuine wisdom.

Buddhism encourages us to confront our higher nature, emphasizing that our true essence is beyond the reach of mere thoughts. Buddhism guides us toward the profound realization of our elevated nature and the wisdom that accompanies it.

LIVING THE WAY OF BUDDHISM: A PATH TO DYNAMIC TRANSFORMATION

Buddhism transcends specific practices; it is fundamentally a way of living life gracefully. Rather than fixating on methodologies, the essence lies in crafting a soulful, truthful, and blissful existence, aligning with the teachings of the Buddha.

Through this mindful way of living, a miraculous and dynamic transformation of self-potential unfolds.

The victory is internal achieved within the mind through a shift in consciousness. This internal triumph imbues you with a warrior spirit, empowering you to approach life with heightened energy and self-composure, embracing a state of true bliss.

Such a dynamic and mindful approach to life paves the way for genuine success and peace of mind, resonating with the essence of Buddhism in its truest sense.

TALK LESS

Buddhism offers a simple yet powerful formula for cultivating deep peace within oneself: *talk less!*

The less one engages in conversation, the less disturbance arises at the level of the mind.

Inner silence begets emotional calmness, quieting the heart and dissolving feelings of ill will toward others. Through this tranquility, a profound and undisturbed peace emerges.

The peace attained through silence fosters a serene internal state and instils an iron-like strength within.

Embracing this timeless wisdom from Buddhism, adopting the practice of talking less, promises great rewards in life—ushering in a sense of profound calmness and inner strength.

TRANSCENDING TIME: UNVEILING TIMELESSNESS IN BUDDHIST MEDITATION

For the true Buddhist, the art of transcending time unfolds in the sacred moment of meditation. Here, one delves into an experience of timelessness, a state of being detached from the linear timescale that governs mankind. Instead, the focus shifts toward attachment to infinity—a space beyond the constraints of ordinary time.

Embracing this sense of timelessness and the boundless nature of infinity bestows a feeling of lightness, lifting away the burdens of worrisome thoughts.

The resulting vibrancy and heightened sense of being come with a deepening connection with the timeless and infinite—an essential aim of Buddhism for those seeking profound inner transformation.

BUDDHIST PRACTICE: CULTIVATING SINGULARITY FOR ENLIGHTENED LIVING

The ultimate goal of Buddhist practice is to foster integration within oneself—a unity of mind and heart propelling one toward Buddhahood. In a world where desires and emotions often pull the mind in different directions, Buddhism grounds individuals in the singular and integrated pursuit of enlightened living.

Enlightened living is the true aim of life. As life's true aim, enlightened living automatically infuses peace, bliss, and strength into the heart and spirit. The central focus on moving toward enlightenment itself becomes a transformative force.

The Buddha illustrated a profound insight

when questioned why more people do not attain enlightenment. He dispatched a person to inquire about people's desires in the village. Upon the person 's return, she shared the multitude of worldly aspirations people desire and wish for—wealth, political power, and more. With discerning wisdom, the Buddha inquired, "But does anyone want to be enlightened?" The disciple's nod indicated otherwise . . .

This tale underscores the importance of embracing the higher goal of enlightened living. It serves as a poignant reminder that setting this elevated aspiration opens the door to limitless possibilities, transcending the conventional pursuits that often distract us from the path of profound self-realization.

THE PATH OF FEARLESSNESS: BUILDING SELF-FAITH IN THE LIGHT OF BUDDHA'S WISDOM

The essence of the Buddha's teachings lies in shedding all fear and doubt, and this journey begins with cultivating unwavering self-faith. Self-faith begins with trust in life, and this makes us walk on fearlessly!

True courage arises from having faith in oneself and the transformative power embedded in the Buddha's path. This faith is not a blind belief, but a sturdy foundation built upon the rock of self-assurance—that you have the potential to attain Buddhahood.

As fear dwindles through self-faith, life transforms into a divine experience full of serene power. New horizons unfold, revealing a greater reality within oneself, and pursuing higher achievements becomes a natural progression on the enlightened path.

THE BUDDHA'S WAY: EMBRACING HUMILITY FOR ETERNAL JOY

Contrary to our innate desire to feel superior, the Buddha's path advocates the annihilation of egoism (*attakāmatā*) and the cultivation of humility (*nihatamānatā*).

True enlightenment lies in cultivating utter humility. This profound humility bestows silent strength, genuine peace, and a sacred perspective on life. It connects us to the infinite, filling our beings with ineffable joy and the eternal power of enlightened living—the true essence of the Buddha's teachings.

Buddhism's Promise: The Unwavering Light Within

Amid life's fluctuating circumstances and the ever-changing tide of emotions, Buddhism assures us that the light within—the essence of the Buddha—is eternally aglow within us. We just have to become conscious of it!

Regardless of our current mood or external conditions, this unwavering light persists, reminding us that our intrinsic power and potential for enlightenment are constant, irrespective of external fluctuations.

Buddhism's profound concept illuminates our connection to an enduring inner power—a perpetual luminosity that never dims. Embracing this perspective in every moment and circumstance leads to great calmness. strength, courage, and faith, transforming challenges into opportunities. It is a simple yet profound way of approaching life, fostering gratitude for the inherent brilliance within.

THE MIND: A DOUBLE-EDGED SWORD IN THE BUDDHIST PERSPECTIVE

According to Buddhism, the mind possesses a sacred and vital role—it acts as a mechanism for questioning, leading us toward truth. Yet, it also has the potential to fabricate untruths, especially fears, anxieties, and hindrances. This duality emphasizes the importance of cultivating self-faith and aligning with the higher vision of our Buddhahood and cosmic connection, minimizing the mind's tendency to lead us astray.

Buddhism advises us not to over rely on the mind's functions. Instead, it encourages us to utilize our minds without becoming enslaved by their many apprehensions.

By avoiding the sway of the mind's uncertainties, we foster a stronger connection with the qualities of the heart—courage, love, trust, faith, and bravery. Embracing these qualities aligns us with the true spirit of the Buddha's calming mystical path.

IN PURSUIT OF ENLIGHTENMENT: OVERCOMING THE EMPEROR OF DELUSION

In Buddhism, 'Mara' symbolizes the mind's delusions, desires, and fears. Mara is also known as the Lord of the Senses, the Lord of Death, the demon-emperor of delusion, and represents evil or dark forces.

Gautam Buddha's final journey toward enlightenment involved overcoming Mara. Buddhist stories highlight how the Buddha remained undistracted by Mara's many sensual temptations and threats, exemplifying the importance of not identifying with the mind's illusions on the path to enlightenment.

In emulating Gautam Buddha's mystical journey, it is essential to learn from this unwavering determination he showed during his final push toward enlightenment. Instead of letting the mind weaken our resolve in any situation, the key lies in cultivating determination from the heart and following the path of inner strength . . . letting nothing come in the way!

EMBODIED GRACE: THE BUDDHA TOUCH IN EVERYDAY ACTIONS

Oriental spiritual paths such as Zen Buddhism and Taoism teach the art of infusing great grace into every task. Witnessing a Zen master engage in mundane activities, like gardening or making tea, reveals an ineffably graceful aura and remarkably calm efficiency.

This ability to bring the Buddha touch to even the smallest actions exemplify the profound impact of grace on our daily lives.

Zen Buddhism teaches that the quality of energy we bring to our actions, the vibrancy within, is the key. This tangible yet intangible essence is the heart of Buddha's path, emphasizing the importance of the quality of being in every action, whether significant or small. It stands as Buddhism's profoundly practical lesson, echoed in the modern age by teachers such as DT Suzuki and Alan Watts

THE POWER OF BLESSING: UNLEASHING LOVE'S HIGHEST ENERGY IN BUDDHISM

In Buddhism, the profound teaching is that our greatest blessing to others comes through the power of our inner peace and love—the highest energies within us.

True Buddhists silently radiate peace and love, which are subtle forces that do not require words or touch. By blessing the world with this peace and love, they elevate their energy to a state of perpetual bliss and calm.

On the Buddhist path, receiving alms was a means of sustenance for monks, while simultaneously, they dedicated their energy to a profound sense of loving blessedness toward the world. This dual dynamic, giving and receiving, transforms not only the lives of others but also blesses and enriches one's existence.

BUDDHIST HARMONY: THE SOFT STRENGTH OF INNER SENSITIVITY

In ancient times, Buddhists engaged in rigorous austerities, yet they were known for their softness and calm sensitivity in their behavior toward others.

This intriguing paradox reflects the beauty of the Buddhist path. While embracing challenging practices, Buddhists cultivate a soft, compassionate, and non-imposing demeanor. In the face of criticism, they respond with a smile, embodying the philosophy that nothing should be taken negatively in the Buddhist vision.

Cultivating the power of patience (*khantibala*) is akin to growing deep roots. The strongest tree withstands life's storms because of its firm connection to the earth through deep roots. You become stronger when your roots are deeper. Then, you can withstand the storms of life. The tree with the deepest roots is indeed the strongest tree - that is the way of Buddhism: be like that.

Dig your roots firmly into the soil—anchor yourself with patience and stand tall like the mighty oak tree—magnificent, silent, gentle yet strong, providing shade to all in need.

INDIVIDUAL ESSENCE IN BUDDHISM

Being a Buddhist involves recognizing and sharing your individual skills within a *sangha* or organization. This, done nobly and unselfishly, allows you to contribute your unique gifts to the collective and the world.

In the vastness of a group, maintaining a connection with your individual skill set fosters a sense of value creation and the ability to make valuable contributions to the collective whole. This leads to a serene sense of service for the greater good.

A true Buddhist embraces both self-reliance and giving, taking responsibility for their growth and development and that of others. This attitude is a foundation for personal strength, excellence, and the ability to support others.

By shouldering responsibilities, the Buddhist path becomes a journey toward personal empowerment, leading to serene excellence in various aspects of life.

CHAPTER 12

Simplicity Elevated: The Profound Meditations in Buddhism

Zen Buddhism advises turning *every* activity into meditation—sitting, walking, working—reflecting the fusion of profundity and simplicity of Buddhist practice. The approach extends beyond formal meditation, encouraging the infusion of mindfulness into daily life, work, and relationships. Buddhism teaches a valuable lesson: turn simplicity into meditative excellence for clarity and calmness in every endeavor.

Buddhism transforms ordinary practices into profound meditations, emphasizing simplicity. Practices like Vipassana and Anapanasati yoga elevate basic acts, such as breath observation, to transformative meditations (the 'Anapanasati Sutta' outlines sixteen methods, grouped into contemplation of the body, feeling, mind, and fostering mindfulness).

Breath awareness, a fundamental mechanism, becomes a primary Buddhist vehicle for profound shifts in consciousness, revealing depth within simplicity.

Zen's *zazen,* an open-eyed witnessing meditation, teaches observing thoughts as passing clouds in the expansive sky of self-realization.

MINDFULNESS ON BREATHING

In Anapanasati yoga, the practice of 'mindfulness on in-and-out-breathing' is pivotal for achieving serene mental concentration and the four absorptions (*jhána*). The Satipatthána Sutta and other texts present sixteen methods categorized into four groups of four, applicable to both tranquillity (*samatha*) and insight meditation. The exercises range from breath awareness to contemplation of impermanence, detachment, extinction, and abandonment.

The Buddha's instructions on mindfulness of in-and-out breathing include these words: "Calming this bodily function I will breathe in; calming this bodily function I will breathe out . . . Feeling joy, I will breathe in; feeling joy, I will breathe out . . . Freeing the mind, I will breathe in; freeing the mind, I will breathe out . . ."

This Buddhist yogas of watching the breath, detailed in the Ánápánasati Sutta, also contribute to the four foundations of mindfulness (*satipatthána*)—contemplation of the body, feeling, and mind. Further, they lead to the development of the seven factors of enlightenment (*bojjhanga*), culminating in the deliverance of mind (*ceto-vimutti*) and deliverance through wisdom (*paññá-vimutti*). The breath becomes the vehicle for calm, joy, liberation and transformation.

EMPOWERING INDIVIDUALITY: BUDDHISM'S EGALITARIAN PATH

Buddhism beautifully combines the concept of group support *along with* the empowerment of individuality. Emphasizing self-reliance, it sees each person as unique and special.

Buddhism fosters self-respect and self-realization by rejecting the notion of one being lesser than another. This concept instills confidence, cultivates leadership skills, and encourages individuals to shine as lights, adding value to the world and guiding others toward positive endeavors.

In a world often swayed by group dynamics and collective thinking, Buddhism's emphasis on recognizing one's unique individuality is a profound lesson. Realizing your distinctive characteristics awakens untapped potential, fostering responsibility and empowerment.

This approach encourages bravery, courage and resilience, equipping individuals to navigate life's diverse challenges with supreme calmness, confidence and resilience.

MINDFULNESS ON PEACE

The quickest way to attain inner peace is *to place one's consciousness on peace* and tranquility. We can do this in several ways:

a. The practice of *upasamánussati*: Recollection of peace, with the consciousness directed toward feelings of peace.

b. Mindfulness on breathing (*anapanasati*)

c. Contemplation upon the Buddha, as the Buddhist scriptures direct us: "When the disciple recollects the Enlightened One, his mind becomes free of greed, hatred, and delusion. The disciple's mind becomes integrated and understands the blissful law. Great bliss arises, with the heart becoming joyous and the mind attaining the stillness of calm. The mind feels happy, steady."

d. Advanced contemplation of death and the body through the practices of marana-sati and káyagatá-sati, respectively, also leads to serenity and wisdom.

CHAPTER 13

Unveiling the Hero's Essence: A Legacy of Selfless Giving Across Cultures

Throughout human history, the hero archetype emerges as a consistent force for societal good, creating enduring value. A defining trait of these true heroes is their engagement with the fullness of being, characterized by a selfless style of functioning rooted in sharing. Distinctively, they operate without a constant desire for reciprocity, working from abundant energy. Whether in oriental or Western literature, this universal principle underscores the authentic hero's journey, leaving a profound legacy of altruism and positive societal impact.

This is in line with Buddhist principles. The lesson is this: Offer the best of your energies selflessly, and you naturally evolve into a beacon of inspiration, a charismatic leader, and a positive example for others.

Embracing the Buddhist principle of sharing energy abundantly becomes a key to creating a significant impact in life. By becoming a good icon through selfless generosity, you inspire others and pave the way for personal and collective growth.

The journey of sharing with complete abundance, rooted in Buddhist ideals, becomes a powerful force propelling you toward profound success, tranquility, and fulfillment.

FORGIVENESS IN BUDDHISM: THE TRANSFORMATIVE TALE OF AṄGULIMĀLA

In Buddhism, forgiveness holds great significance. The story of Aṅgulimāla exemplifies this theme as he transformed from a notorious murderer to a devoted disciple of Buddha.

Despite his dark past, Aṅgulimāla chose repentance and sought forgiveness, experiencing a complete change of heart in the presence of Buddha.

Although he faced punishment in some villages and was stoned, beaten, Aṅgulimāla's remarkable forgiveness toward his attackers deeply moved Buddha.

This tale encourages us to follow Aṅgulimāla's example and highlights the profound power of forgiveness even in life's most challenging moments.

Forgiveness is the key to progress in life, providing us with dynamism.

Buddha's reconciliation with his father is a powerful example, bringing profound peace to his father's heart. Seeking forgiveness is integral to achieving harmony within ourselves, allowing our energy to flow in new directions.

In Buddhist thought, forgiving others is a fundamental principle, emphasizing its transformative impact on our journey toward inner peace and positive energy.

BUDDHISM: TRANSFORMING ENERGY FOR HARMONY

Buddhism is the art of transforming energies.

Gautam Buddha turned his personal sorrow into a message to eliminate humanity's sorrows. He also transformed the energy of his lonely path into a powerful message of harmony by creating the Sangha, the world's largest religious movement at that time. As Buddha said, "Peace comes from within. Do not seek it without."

In life, like in Buddhism, we must transform our energies. Even in moments of sorrow or loneliness, we should not lose hope.

Instead, see these moments as opportunities to achieve something greater in life. This is the essence of Buddhist excellence, as the path to higher achievements often unfolds from the challenges we encounter.

BUDDHIST WISDOM: TRANSFORMING DESPAIR INTO OPTIMISM

Buddhism offers beautiful metaphors for turning moments of despair into uplifting experiences.

One metaphor compares our low moments to the night, emphasizing that there is a sunrise after every night. This encourages us to maintain optimism, even in the darkest times.

As a Buddhist saying goes, "Thousands of candles can be lit from a single candle, and the life of the candle will not be shortened. Happiness never decreases by being shared."

Embrace optimism, channel your energies into calmness, and meditate during challenging times.

In Buddhism, another metaphor likens life's challenges to the process of obtaining pure gold.

Just as gold must go through fire to become pure; we face challenging circumstances.

The key lesson is that after enduring the metaphorical fire, what remains is pure 24 karat gold.

Therefore, never fear moments of solitude; rise above them in your thoughts, knowing that, like refined gold, you will emerge stronger and more resilient.

BUDDHISM: BEYOND IDEOLOGIES, EMBRACING SELF-DISCOVERY

Karl Marx once called religion the opium of the masses. Indeed, religions are often so, and are rigid too. Yet Buddhism stands apart: it is not about imposing rigid ideologies, but is a way of being with awareness and insight. It encourages freedom of consciousness to discover one's true self through meditative awareness. In Buddhism, life is viewed as an opportunity to find our truth and embrace our serene Buddha nature. As Buddhism emphasizes, "Do not be led by others; awaken your mind, amass your own experience, and decide for yourself your path."

To grasp Buddhism's teachings, always remember to break free from ideologies and cultivate clarity of perception. This brings great calmness.

Whether you actively practice Buddhism or integrate its principles into your life, focusing on a clear perspective is key.

This practice, aligned with the path of the Buddha, can impact your actions. It cleanses you of rigid ideologies, fostering creativity and productivity in your endeavors. As Buddhism teaches, "Your work is to discover your world and then with all your heart give yourself to it."

THE DUAL NATURE
OF HUMAN EXISTENCE

Gautam Buddha once reflected on the profound gift of human life, emphasizing its unique position in the vast cosmos. In his teachings, he conveyed the idea that human existence encompasses both profound suffering and immense joy. As beings capable of experiencing such extremes, humans possess the potential to transcend these states. The Buddha envisioned a path to perfect equanimity, freedom from attachments, and the ultimate enlightenment that brings universal illumination.

In contemplating the broader cosmic order, Gautam Buddha acknowledged the existence of higher beings in elevated realms. However, he observed that their perpetual happiness might hinder them from experiencing the essential sorrow that propels individuals toward the enlightened state of a Buddha. On the contrary, in the lower realms, where suffering prevails, aspiring toward enlightenment becomes a formidable challenge. As the Buddha succinctly said, "Life is a great gift, and within the interplay of suffering and joy, we find the transformative path toward ultimate liberation."

Reflecting on the profound teachings of the Buddha, it becomes clear that we should cherish our lives, placing a higher value on their inherent worth. Trusting in the unfolding of life, we are urged to use this precious existence to uncover our Buddha nature—the essence of true excellence and the ultimate success in the perspective of Buddhism.

CHAPTER 14

Inner Serenity: Unveiling Profound Insights from Buddha to Einstein

Life's profound answers gently unfold in the serene sanctuary of inner peace. This tranquil state has been the fertile ground for the most significant revelations throughout human civilization. Consider Gautam Buddha, who attained profound tranquility, unlocking higher truths and achieving Buddhahood. In the scientific realm, Albert Einstein, finding inspiration in moments of absolute relaxation, notably through the harmonious strains of Mozart and Bach, attributed his insights to this unique ease.

Einstein's acknowledgment of the transformative influence of great composers reveals a peculiar state of relaxed awareness fostered by diverse activities. This state, marked by a silent and quiet mind in deep peace, becomes the conduit through which existence imparts answers.

"Cultivate this deep peace within you," echoes the wisdom, inviting you to embrace this state of tranquil awareness. Doing so opens the door to an influx of creative insights, propelling you toward excellence in every endeavor.

CULTIVATING PATIENCE

Cultivating infinite patience is among the Buddha's greatest virtues, symbolizing a profound quality in Buddhism.

The belief that patience leads to positive outcomes while impatience triggers negative consequences resonate not only in the broader world but also on an individual level. Reflect on your life, and you will find that moments of patience have led to significant achievements, while impatience may have caused stumbling.

As the Buddha teaches, patience does not negate ambition or the desire for enlightenment; it coexists with a deep thirst for spiritual growth.

The hunger for higher truth and self-realization should be steadfast, yet practicing patience becomes key in worldly matters.

Patient speech and attentive listening pave the way for swift and effective actions. Embrace and nurture this quality, for in the harmony of patience, you discover the path to achieving great things in both the spiritual and worldly realms.

THE NOBLE ONE

The Buddha, often hailed as the noble one, embodies an essence of infinite nobility.

Emulating this noble quality in our own lives transforms us, elevating our character. The path to nobility unfolds when we transcend egoism, adopt a sharing attitude, and generously offer our inner richness—be it inner bliss, peace, or the light of our energy—to others. Acts of service, inwardly and outwardly, contribute to developing a noble mind and heart.

Striving for nobility is not about seeking respect; it is a natural byproduct of genuine selflessness and sharing.

The Buddha and his noble disciples exemplified this principle, their mere presence commanded respect.

Similarly, cultivating self-respect and embracing the nobility within yourself leads to a spontaneous outpouring of respect from the world.

It is not a pursuit for external validation but a harmonious alignment that naturally draws admiration and respect from those around you.

THE CONCEPT OF BEAUTY
IN ZEN BUDDHISM

Zen Buddhism stands as a distinctive spiritual journey, for it encourages us to perceive the infinite beauty woven into life and the universe itself.

While many religions often focus on the realization of God or truth, Buddhism, especially in the Zen tradition, emphasizes the path that instills a deep appreciation for profound beauty, leading to deep serenity and peacefulness.

In Zen, the experience of beauty becomes a gateway to the spontaneous realization of truth.

This unique perspective is reflected in the creativity of Zen practitioners, leading to the creation of remarkable poetry like "Haiku," intricate art and painting, and aesthetic ceremonies, such as the renowned tea ceremony.

Every aspect of Zen arts, including disciplines like swordsmanship and calligraphy, radiates beauty.

Zen Buddhism echoes the sentiments expressed by the great Indian poet Rabindranath Tagore, who the Buddha profoundly influenced.

Also, John Keats' famous words, "Beauty is truth, truth beauty," find resonance in Zen.

The call to realize more beauty in life is not just an aesthetic pursuit but a path to a richly rewarding existence, as life responds in myriad beautiful ways to those who appreciate its intrinsic beauty.

FINDING POSITIVITY

Often, people think that Buddhism is a life-negative religion because it tells us to renounce things and so on. But Buddha was not life negative at all. In fact, he is the most life-positive person in the history of human civilization. All that he wanted was to go past our illusions about peace of mind and happiness. He wanted us to go past a false sense of joy and move toward true joy, which is only found when we move toward enlightened living.

The alchemy of greater awareness within you brings about true calmness and happiness. The more aware and awake you become in life, the more you move toward greater serenity, truth, higher consciousness, and happiness.

THE SEER

The Buddha is one who sees all things. He is the ultimate seer. He sees deep within you, into your deepest potential.

And all that the Buddha wants is for you to realize your potential. And how is the potential realized?

Self-potential is realized by us through enhancing our ability to see things as they are.

When you see things more deeply, you develop insight or Pragya into the true nature of things. And when you develop insight into things, you automatically become far more calmly capable, creative, and productive.

And then all that you do has a deeper touch, a more valuable touch. You become a value creator in the world.

MEDITATION DYNAMICS

The meditation postures of Buddhists reveal a journey toward complete innocence, akin to the purity of one's state in the mother's womb.

By allowing thoughts to pass without entanglement, practitioners tap into the dynamism of Buddha, guiding them back to a fresh, innocent mindset.

This return to innocence fosters the development of a profound completeness of energy reminiscent of a tightly wound spring ready to unleash tremendous force.

Meditation and Buddhist breathing techniques are tools for renewing energy, relaxing the various energy centers within the body.

This process enables a vibrant and dynamic movement in the world, inviting individuals to increasingly identify with a state of restful energy— an alternate expression for the profound practice of meditation.

BUDDHA'S RADIANCE

While the Buddha is linked with superconscious wisdom, meeting him would have evoked an ineffable and boundless love. Alongside this love, an infinite energy of compassion permeated his being.

In reality, these aspects hold greater significance than what is conventionally deemed wisdom. The Buddha's love, compassion, and awareness are the sources from which wisdom naturally flows. His wisdom transcends knowledge, embodying a deeper, intuitive understanding that emerges from the core of profound love and compassion.

The Buddha's personality was alive with profound love, compassion, and awareness, serving as the true fount of wisdom in life.

Cultivating these qualities, integral to the Buddha's path and encapsulated in the eightfold path of right conduct, leads to a byproduct of excellence, productivity, and happiness in one's life.

Embracing love, compassion, and awareness becomes the seed of greatness, propelling individuals toward greater fulfillment, peace of mind, and success.

BUDDHA'S HUMILITY: A HUMAN PATH TO GODLIKE VIRTUES

While the Buddha never claimed divinity or encouraged others to see him as a god, his godlike qualities emerged naturally. Later Buddhist references elevated him to a god's status, yet his greatness lies in consistently asserting his humanity.

By emphasizing calmness, egolessness, positive life energy, and graceful living, the Buddha conveyed that anyone could embody these virtues. He advocated a spiritual life without imposing the idea of God, urging individuals to explore meditation and delve into self-awareness.

The Buddha's teachings inspire us to embrace our shared humanity, fostering a sense of serenity, beauty, grace, and productivity as fellow citizens on this life journey.

CHAPTER 15

Diverse Dimensions of Buddhahood: Lessons from the Laughing Buddha

I n Buddhism, the term "Buddha" transcends specific individuals and represents a state of being. One notable manifestation is the Laughing Buddha, who imparts profound lessons in merriment, unbridled joy, and the meditative power of laughter.

In contrast to Gautam Buddha, the Laughing Buddha's unique teachings encourage embracing an attitude of laughter and smiling, highlighting that even moments of pure joy can serve as a form of meditation.

This distinctive lesson underscores the diverse facets of Buddhahood and the varied paths toward spiritual enlightenment.

While formal sitting meditation may not appeal to everyone, sharing joy, laughter, and embracing natural delight can be a powerful means of enriching our lives and assisting others on their journeys by generating positive energy.

The essence lies in the belief that we can embody Buddhahood uniquely.

Whether through serene sitting meditation or the uplifting practice of laughter meditation, we can choose to find our distinctive way of expressing our highest energies and contributing to the well-being of all.

MATERIALISM

So many rich people came to Buddha during his lifetime to seek guidance from him to enrich their lives meaningfully.

There are Buddhist stories about rich merchants making great arrangements for the Sangha (Buddha's spiritual commune) in places like Rajgir, Vaishali, etc. Yet the poorest of the poor also came to Buddha.

For the Buddha, there was no distinction between rich and poor. His only distinction was between those people who are moving toward their Buddhahood—who are feeling the joy of serenely enlightened living—and those who are not feeling the joy of enlightened living.

The irony is that most of the rich people did not feel the joy of enlightened living. They were finding it difficult to follow the way of the Buddha, whereas those who did not have much at all, or may have been poor, often found immense joy, great bliss and the serenity in enlightened living.

So, the Buddha's example teaches us that it is not a possession that gives meaning to life. It is something else; that is why Buddha's path is so meaningful. It does not discriminate based on any materialism or any position of power.

It only tells us that it is our choice whether we want to walk upon the noble path of his and experience the true delight of spiritual living or continue hankering after materialism as if it is the end.

BEYOND MATERIALISM: FINDING SERENE EXCELLENCE THROUGH INNER GUIDANCE

Materialism, while a potential starting point for serving the world, can never be the ultimate goal. True satisfaction and serenity arise when guided by the inner Buddha within your heart. Following the voice of your heart, the higher voice of the Buddha within leads to a path of excellence—wherein fulfillment emanates from within, influencing all aspects of your life and allowing excellence to flow effortlessly through your actions.

THE HALF-SECOND GATEWAY: TAPPING INTO INNER EXCELLENCE

Closing our eyes for just half a second allows us to connect with the Buddha within, unlocking the divinely peaceful and powerful energy residing within ourselves!

Encouraging frequent moments of internal introspection, this practice offers a remedy for anxiety and worry. We access vast reservoirs of bliss, calm, creative productivity, and self-potential realization by going within.

Cultivating this habit brings forth confidence, courage, relaxation, and positive energy, empowering us to excel in the external world and navigate life with excellence—a simple yet profound secret to inner and outer fulfillment.

THE PATH OF THE BRAVE: SCALING INNER PEAKS WITH BUDDHA'S WISDOM

The path of the Buddha is not for the faint-hearted; it requires true courage and strength. To embark on this journey means being bold and driven toward higher living and loftier goals. While ordinary goals most often lead nowhere in terms of achieving serene enlightenment, following the Buddha demands a daring exploration of one is potential for serenely enlightened living.

The irony is that humanity often attempts to

conquer external mountains but hesitates to scale the inner summit where the Buddha resides. According to Buddhism, real success begins by realizing one's inner capacities. Acknowledging one's potential is the first step toward achieving it.

Buddhism encourages the exploration and realization of one's inner capacities. As one actualizes these capacities, external success, peace of mind, and calmness naturally follow.

CHAPTER 16

Buddhism and
The Tightrope Walker:
The Art of Balance

Imagine a tightrope walker in action—
that is the essence of Buddhism.
Walking the rope represents the path
where maintaining balance is key.

Buddhism is about avoiding extremes,
like the walker who stays neither too hot

nor too cold in his temperament, instead holding a steady and calm mind.

In Buddhism, this is referred to as the middle path, emphasizing the art of balance as the crux of the entire philosophy.

Just like a tightrope walker navigating with precision, cultivating a calm and meditative mind is fundamental to walking the path of the Buddha.

In maintaining perfect balance, relaxation coexists attentively to the present moment, much like the tightrope walker who does not dwell on the past or future.

Embracing the present with a relaxed yet profoundly aware mind symbolizes the essence of Buddhism. When mastered, this art leads to a genuine state of excellence in mind, body, and spirit, offering a pathway to holistic well-being.

CULTIVATING ETERNAL BEAUTY WITHIN

While human obsession often fixates on external beauty's transient nature, Buddhism emphasizes the enduring allure of internal beauty.

Recognizing that all external beauty is subject to change, Buddhism advocates for cultivating inner beauty—an art that spans lifetimes. By nurturing inner feelings of beauty, one embarks on the path of the Buddha, discovering the profound and lasting beauty that resides within, transcending the ephemeral nature of external appearances.

This creates great calm, serenity, composure and rootedness.

Just as the Buddha aged in body but retained a youthful spirit, we too should cultivate an undisturbed and non-distracted state within ourselves.

By maintaining inner tranquility, we strive toward a state akin to the Buddha. This timeless beauty transcends the external aging of the body and reflects the enduring youthfulness of the heart and spirit.

SILENT SERENITY: UNVEILING THE TRUE PRAYER IN ANCIENT BUDDHISM

In the early days of original Buddhism, prayer to deities was absent; instead, Buddhists delved into a form of meditativeness that transcended words—embracing profound silence.

They discovered that true prayer resides in quietude. Achieving this serene state ensures that all prayers are answered without pleading with existence. It calls for surrender, a laying aside of ego, and in this humble stance, all desires are generously provided.

It is said: "The answer to every prayer is hidden within the silence of your heart, where the whispers of wisdom are heard."

In the pursuit of material achievement, too, the wisdom of detachment holds true. Those committed to creating value in the world focus on their endeavors without fixating on so-called short-term results. The challenge lies not in the short-term outcomes but in the tension spawned by the small result-oriented mindset. Buddhism encourages an expanded, open mindset.

Remember to do this:

Relax your being, saying to yourself that whatever you do will be for good. Then, you will automatically be of value to the world because all your acts will be creative, compassionate, love, and concern for others.

TRUE LEADERSHIP: IN THE FOOTSTEPS OF THE BUDDHA

Following in Gautam Buddha's footsteps, countless individuals were drawn to his spiritual leadership, recognizing his heightened wakefulness and enlightenment. This signifies the essence of true leadership—the ability to display greater awareness and instill wakefulness.

The ultimate law of leadership unfolds organically when authenticity is embraced; there is no need for falsehoods. A true leader is deeply committed to their self-truth, inspiring belief, and voluntary followership through sincerity and genuine dedication.

Enlightened leaders do not emerge from positions of power or wealth; they are born out of inner clarity.

True leadership arises from an inward calm, tranquility, and self-realization. When one is inwardly collected, possessing inner charisma, others instinctively look up to them.

In today's world, where ethical leadership is crucial yet lacking in various fields, this often-overlooked aspect must be emphasized.

Whether in politics, business, or religion, the path of the Buddha offers a timeless guide toward genuine and impactful leadership.

Discovering Happiness Within: The Heart of Buddha's Wisdom

The Buddha teaches that the root of human unhappiness is not recognizing our inherent joyous nature, Buddhahood. Embracing one's inner Buddhahood dispels unhappiness, simplifying Buddhism's core message.

The teaching emphasizes looking within, urging a conscious remembrance of this truth without being swayed by life's illusions. Everything sought lies within oneself, free from egoistic beliefs or religious supremacy.

In Buddhism, nothing is seen as inherently sacred or profane. It guides a journey of self-realization, revealing the simplicity of truth within. Buddhism revolves around self-awareness and identifying with the inherent beauty of one is being.

It is a straightforward path, promoting spontaneity. Letting go of the past and detaching from future outcomes defines its essence. Realizing the self in the present moment brings forth hidden potentials, making one stronger, wiser, and more dynamic in actions.

BUDDHISM'S EGALITARIAN WISDOM: NURTURING CONFIDENCE BEYOND COMPARISONS

In our materialistic world, many feel they lack the skills or talents to thrive professionally. Buddhism, however, offers a profound perspective—Buddhahood requires no unique skills or exceptional talents; it is innate within us.

This teaching rejects the materialistic practice of comparison, embracing an egalitarian system where everyone is equal. No negative self-perceptions or feelings of inferiority are warranted; we are equal to those with exceptional skills.

Recognizing this equality fosters confidence, facilitates the realization of our inherent potential, guides us toward self-realization, and imparts valuable lessons for our psychological well-being.

Buddhism transcends religious boundaries, functioning as a psychological science of consciousness. By addressing issues like the inferiority complex, it becomes a powerful tool for healing. Its practical significance lies in dispelling such negative feelings, fostering a sense of capability in line with our inherent potential, enabling profound personal growth and well-being.

THE SILENCE OF BUDDHA: EMBRACING NO-MIND FOR PROFOUND TRANQUILITY

It is said that the Buddha stepped out of the mind and entered a state of complete no-mind—a profound silence and infinite calm.

Even a Buddha statue evokes this silence, this calm- free from the energy of restless thought.

Within the Buddha, energy is pure, innocent, compassionate, loving, and powerful. It is infinitely deep and comes from a great height of feeling, devoid of thought.

Embracing the Buddha's way, we, too, must delve into pure feeling and experience the tremendous divine essence of no thought.

In mystical parlance, life is to be approached as a play, a series of acts. This demands a surrender of our thoughts and mental chatter. Freedom from constant mental chatter leads us to sense the state of the Buddha. And through that intuition, one finds great peace, internal power, happiness, restful productivity, and creativity simultaneously. Emulating the way of the Buddha brings profound benefits.

THE BUDDHA'S MEDITATION: A LESSON FOR ALL

People often wonder about the Buddha's continued meditation after achieving enlightenment. His ongoing practice was solely to set an example for others. Despite having transcended the need for meditation himself, the Buddha continued to meditate in the presence of his disciples, emphasizing the importance of their relentless pursuit of the path to Buddhahood.

His actions were a guiding lesson for the enduring energy needed in meditation.

The more you dig, the more treasures you will find—a profound example set by the Buddha. As a true mystic leader, he continued walking the path even after reaching the proverbial summit or Mt Everest of mystic realization—i.e., the pinnacle of freedom or nirvana.

To emphasize his lessons, he showed us that the pursuit and refinement of the bliss of Buddhahood must continue ever onward!

The determination of the Buddha serves as an inspiring example, encouraging us to go on, embodying the true essence of meditation.

BREAKING FREE FROM CONDITIONED THOUGHTS: THE BUDDHA'S LIBERATION PATH

Our years of education and societal upbringing often strengthen our negative thinking, contrary to the belief that they make us better people.

The Buddhist path aims to break the conditioned patterns of negative thoughts and take us toward a serenely free mindset.

The Buddha's way is to cut through what we know, bringing us to a clear state of consciousness—a journey at the heart of meditation.

Meditation, as taught by the Buddha, transcends traditional sitting practices. It stands for cultivating the right thoughts and right attitudes.

In its true essence, Buddhist meditation involves cutting down all past conditioning and entering a space where the mind is fresh, new, and free to perceive rightly. This is the core of right thought in the Buddhist sense, and from right thought emerges right action.

Cultivate this, and you will unlock infinite peace, creativity, and excellence in life.

EMBRACING INNER DEPTH: LESSONS FROM THE BUDDHA

The Buddha faced formidable enemies, like his own cousin Devadatta, who sought to harm him, yet he remained undisturbed. His profound depth shielded him from surface disturbances. Learning from the Buddha, we too can delve into our inner depths, cultivating a fearlessness that shields us from anxiety, wavering thoughts, and external disturbances.

It is all about cultivating inner power, through which comes fearlessness.

The Buddha taught that human courage is not a façade; it emerges naturally when we explore our immeasurable depth. Fear dissolves as we uncover this inner reservoir, leaving us unshakable, relaxed, and authentically powerful.

Embracing these lessons unleashes the inherent fearlessness that resides within us. It keeps us perfectly centered, composed centered, composed, and calm in life's various situations.

Om gate gate paragate
Parasamgate bodhi svaha.
Gone, gone, gone beyond, utterly beyond . . .
What a profound awakening . . . all praise!

Mantra from the Heart Sutra,
Mahayana Buddhism

Acknowledgments

I would like to express my sincere gratitude to the individuals who have played a pivotal role in bringing this series to life: Anuj Bahri, my exceptional literary agent at Red Ink; Gaurav Sabharwal and Shantanu Duttagupta, my outstanding publishers at Fingerprint! Publishing, along with their dedicated team. Special thanks to Shilpa Mohan, my editor for her invaluable contributions.

I would also like to extend my heartfelt appreciation to my parents, Anita and Captain Jeet Gupta, for their unwavering support throughout this journey. To my beloved sister, Priti and brother-in-law, Manish Goel, thank you for always being there for me. My niece, Vaanee and nephew, Kartikay have been a constant source of joy and inspiration and I am grateful for their presence in my life.

I am truly humbled by the collective efforts and encouragement from all these remarkable individuals, without whom this series would not have been possible.

Pranay is a renowned mystic, captivating speaker and accomplished author who has dedicated his life to exploring the depths of spirituality. With a deep understanding of the human experience and an unwavering commitment to personal growth, Pranay has written numerous books that offer insights into the realms of spirituality.

One of Pranay's most celebrated contributions is his groundbreaking series of modules titled "Advanced Spirituality for Leadership and Success." His transformative PowerTalks and MysticTalks have garnered international recognition for their exceptional ability to inspire and empower individuals from all walks of life. Pranay's unique approach combines ancient wisdom with contemporary insights, providing a roadmap for achieving spiritual fulfillment while embracing leadership qualities that lead to remarkable success.

To learn more about Pranay and his transformative teachings, visit his official website at pranay.org.

To buy more books by the author scan the QR code given below.